Mr. Wolf
Leaves Town

Written by Sarah Prince
Illustrated by Peter Paul Bajer

We are the three little pigs,
and we have a plan.

We plan to frighten
the big, bad wolf.

SECRET PLAN

"Mr. Wolf! Mr. Wolf!
It's time to leave town.

Mr. Wolf! Mr. Wolf!
I'll knock your house down.

Mr. Wolf! Mr. Wolf!
Open the door!

Or I'll huff, and I'll puff,
and knock it flat to the floor,"
shouted one little pig.

The wolf looked out the window.

He saw one little pig and laughed.

"Mr. Wolf! Mr. Wolf!
It's time to leave town.

Mr. Wolf! Mr. Wolf!
We'll knock your house down.

Mr. Wolf! Mr. Wolf!
Open the door!

Or we'll bash, and we'll crash,
and knock it flat to the floor,"
shouted two little pigs.

9

The wolf looked out the window.

He saw two little pigs and laughed
and laughed.

"That wolf is not worried.
That wolf does not care.

We'll have to work harder
to give him a scare."

"Mr. Wolf! Mr. Wolf!
It's time to leave town.

Mr. Wolf! Mr. Wolf!
We'll knock your house down.

Mr. Wolf! Mr. Wolf!
Open the door!

Or we'll bang, and we'll clang,
and knock it flat to the floor."

The wolf looked out the window,
and he saw ...

15

"AAGH!"

The three little pigs laughed and laughed and laughed.